Three Good Things

Happiness Every Day, No Matter What!

ERIKA K. OLIVER

IN THE AFFIRMATIVE PUBLISHING
PORTAGE, MI

Three Good Things
Happiness Every Day, No Matter What!

by Erika K. Oliver

Published by:

> In The Affirmative Publishing
> PMB 239
> 271-A W. Centre
> Portage MI 49024

> Printed in the United States of America

Publisher's Cataloging-in-Publication Data

Oliver, Erika K.
  Three Good Things: happiness every day, no matter what / Erika K.
  Oliver. -- Portage, Mich. : In the Affirmative Publishing, 2nd ed., 2007.
  p. ; cm.
  ISBN-13: 978-0-9799025-1-2

  1. Happiness. 2. Attitude (Psychology) 3. Gratitude. 4. Quality of
life. 5. Positive Communication. I. Title.

Book layout: **Andrea Stork**
Editing: **Jeanne Wenz**
Author photo: **Patricia Schneider**

Dedication

Believing my professional life was merely in a temporary lull, I took a job as a teacher at a technical school because I needed work. Little did I know I would discover my life's passion. I am so grateful for that difficult time in my career because I would never have experienced the absolute joy I feel when I teach.

This book is dedicated to all the students who have participated in my classes—at the community college, at the Chamber of Commerce, in business and professional organizations, and in workshops.

My passion to teach has only grown. Thank you for inspiring me to share *Three Good Things* and for your feedback on how it positively affected your life. Because of you, I came to more fully understand the significance of *Three Good Things* and am taking your advice to share this powerful exercise with as many people as possible.

Acknowledgements

For Mark, Erik, and Evan—you've made my life what it is. I never thought I was "mom" or "wife" material, and you gave me a place to become someone more than I ever thought I could be. Every day is an adventure with you and I am so grateful.

For my mom and my dad, for living their own struggles and owning their lives. I am just beginning to understand who you are and appreciate what you've given me.

For my creative and beautiful friends: Sarah, Diana, Ronda, Sheryl, Brenda and Kathleen. Thank you for your gifts to the world and for loving me in my imperfect state.

For Andy, my brilliant graphic designer, and Jeanne, my masterful editor, without you this edition would not have been possible. You both brought this work to a new level.

Contents

Introduction 8

Chapter 1: Labeling: Good Versus Bad 13

Chapter 2: Selecting Your Vanishing Point 21

Chapter 3: What Goes into a Bad Day 29

Chapter 4: What Makes Any Day a Good Day 37

Chapter 5: *Three Good Things* about the Day: My Story 45

Chapter 6: *Three Good Things*: Opening Up Possibilities 59

Chapter 7: *Three Good Things:* In All Aspects of Your Life 69

Chapter 8: *Three Good Things*: At Work 85

Chapter 9: Choosing Only Good Days 97

Three Good Things Example Lists 104

Ideas for When and How to Use *Three Good Things* 110

Endnote 113

Erika's Recommended Reading 115

Creative Workshops 116

About the Author 120

Introduction

When my husband and I moved from our first house—a two-bedroom bungalow—to our second home with more room for our family, we sorted through our things as people do when they move. Our two-drawer metal filing cabinet held some important papers, but mostly a lot of junk. In sorting, I found an envelope with writing on the back. It looked like an envelope that was emptied of a utility bill and then used as scrap paper. The writing was mine, and it was a list.

On the list were all the things we wanted in our lives—if we could have anything. I remember how we talked about what we wanted and fantasized about our "ideal" life in the areas of career, finances, friends, and family. Being a seasoned goal setter, I knew the power of writing down goals, so down they were written on the first piece of paper available. But then that emptied bill envelope with the list of our dreams wound up in the two-drawer filing cabinet. I would never have been able to locate it if I had not been cleaning out the files to lighten our move.

The list included:

- Erika finishes her Bachelor's degree
- Mark gets a job at the corporation where he's been interviewing
- Erika works part time
- We have a baby
- We move to a bigger house
- Mark competes in 5K races

That was the extent of the work we had done on our goal setting—fantasizing, writing it down on the back of a bill envelope, and shoving it into a drawer. It startled me that five items had happened or were happening. I had a Bachelor's in Business Administration, Mark had landed his dream job, our son was two years old, Mark finished his most recent 5K race in 19 minutes, and we were moving to a bigger home. It amazed me that all of this happened without much effort. I showed the envelope to my husband and we scratched our heads. Thinking back, we traced our accomplishments to when we began our practice of sharing *Three Good Things* about our day with each other.

Since then, I have been able to work part time, and not just at any part-time job, but as a self-employed business consultant, speaker and trainer. It wasn't a straight line that I followed to my current schedule, but a journey that included full-time work, part-time work for an employer, and assorted freelance jobs.

I began telling the *Three Good Things* story in training sessions to illustrate the power of perspective and positive expectations. The people in the room would get very quiet as I told my story and would approach me after and share how valuable it was for them to hear it. On evaluations, *Three Good Things* would consistently be written under, "most important thing I learned". This happened whether the topic was marketing, planning, decision making, or nonprofit management. After people practiced *Three Good Things*, they encouraged me to write and talk this powerful happiness tool.

The *Three Good Things* story itself is in Chapter 5. The preceding chapters provide background on the philosophy and ideas that support *Three Good Things*. The chapters following the story are written about the application and daily practice of this philosophy and exercise. This "More Good Things" edition adds my newest experiences with *Three Good Things* and input from readers. A new chapter, "*Three Good Things* at Work" has been added because work is where my initial public application of the exercise began and readers have asked for more support in applying the exercise to the professional portion of their lives.

Each chapter begins with *Three Good Things* about the chapter, and ends with an example of my own *Three Good Things* and a place to share yours. With everything I teach, I feel a responsibility to make sure it is grounded in reality—I don't mean what you or I believe to be true, but the reality of how to apply new ideas and practices within our current lives.

If I teach you something great and you are not physically or emotionally able to incorporate the information, then how great is it really? In my thinking, it's not so valuable. But what is great about *Three Good Things* is that it is an easy fit into any part of anyone's life. You will feel an immediate shift to a more positive energy which is the best place from which to think, make decisions and take action.

Labeling: Good Versus Bad

Three Good Things...
About Labels

1. Labels are your choice

2. All things contain both "good" and "bad"

3. Choosing "good" *is* an option, no matter what is happening

Today I look at my high school identification badge and marvel at how pretty I was, while every day during high school I berated myself for eating "bad" food and being fat. How I wished I was pretty, and popular, and athletic. From my adult viewpoint, I see the beauty, remember my friends, and appreciate the awkward and turbulent teenage adventures. It occurs to me that my experiences of high school haven't changed; my perspective is different.

From an adult perspective, doesn't high school always look good? While I was experiencing high school, it seemed bad to me even though I look at it much differently now. Recently, two high school peers, classmates though not particularly friends of mine, shared with me their vision of how I appeared in those long-ago days. They saw me as thin, pretty and well liked. What a shock to me. Go figure! How could I have been so wrong about myself?

"Good" and "bad" are labels arbitrarily applied to food, people, actions, and experiences depending on one's value system and interpretation at that moment. It seems that the labels of "good" and "bad" are specific definitions. However, when derived from a personal perspective they become gray and subjective. Thus when applied to a food experience, for example, I might label a meal as "bad," whereas your perception might label it as "good". Similarly, what I might consider a "good" relationship might be considered "bad" by your standards.

I am not saying there is no "good" or "bad," but both are judgments under our control, based on our subjective experience in present time. We can choose the label "good" right now, even before we know what happens next. We do not have to wait until years later to declare that a day, time, or event in our life was better than it appeared to be in the moment as I did when I looked at an early photo of myself. In hind-sight my label is totally different from the opinion I held at the time it was taken.

Judgements are part of the syndrome of getting caught up in the melodrama of daily life and being dependent on a specific outcome or outside sources of approval. By hastily attaching the label "bad" to events, days and circumstances, we miss out on the joy and excitement of the adventure as it happens. I, for one, do not want to wait for years to experience all of my "good" days. Applying a label of "good" without having to know what happens next is life affirming. Applying a label of "bad" in the same situation sets one up for regret.

Complicating the fact that "good" and "bad" are subjective labels is the fact that, in most cases, "good" and "bad" are intertwined. In a few instances they may seem independent of each other and easy to assign—broccoli is bad, candy is good. But, in thinking about it, our certainty loses its crispness. The taste of broccoli may be "bad" to you, but you can agree that its nutrients are "good" for your health. On the other hand, candy tastes, "good" but it's "bad" for your heart and hips.

In the movies, life is accompanied by music that shifts with the characters' experiences and as their emotions and moods change. When the theme song from Jaws plays, you know that something "bad" is or will be happening. When a romantic songs plays, you know you will be watching something "good" like romance or at least a little lust. Perhaps we all need a sound track to run during different times of our life. I choose to start each day with "Brick House" by the Commodores to boost my self-esteem and revel in the fact that I enjoy what I see in my mirror, whether that image conforms to a specific culture's description of the "ideal" or not!

What sound track will you choose? I think I'll end my day in a peaceful, relaxing way with a Lionel Ritchie love ballad, maybe "Just to Be Close to You". It would remind me that no matter what is happening in my work, or any other theatre of my life, it's my twenty-year marriage that matters. I invite you to find a piece of your life of which you are grateful, and choose an appropriate lyric, melody or both.

"Good" and "bad" are part of everything. Your job, your relationships, and even your opinion of today's weather are both "good" and "bad." Fortunately, it's not a win/lose predicament, but an option, depending on how you view your circumstances. Choosing your viewpoint—your perspective—allows you to determine the balance of "good" and "bad" in your life, no matter what happens or how others might label your day or the experience. And, in the absence of a personal sound track as your guide, choosing "good" as a label most of the time is your best bet. If you believe that "it's all good," then good will come even if it's in the form of a tough lesson learned.

Three things I choose to label "good" that might not appear to be are: birthdays, bills and tight clothes.

On my birthday I am the youngest I will be all year. Hey, since it's my birthday, maybe someone will buy lunch for me! What I learned from Louise Hay, author of many wonderful books on the power of gratitude and positive thinking, is that bills are a sign that creditors believe you have the ability to pay. The fit of my clothes reminds me to pay attention to what I am eating and how much I am exercising to maintain the size that I worked hard to achieve. As someone who used to be eighty pounds heavier, tight clothes *are* a gift.

How about you? What are three things that you choose to label "good" that you might previously have labeled "bad"? Remember, everything has both attributes; your label is a matter of choice.

Three Things I Choose to Label "Good"

1. My birthday

2. Paying bills

3. Tight clothes

Three Things You Choose to Label "Good"

1. Music

2. Haircuts

3. mowing the lawn

Selecting Your Vanishing Point

Three Good Things... ## About Perspective

1. You are the artist of your perspective

2. You choose your vanishing point

3. Adjustments are part of the journey

Using perspective techniques is a skill that beginning art students learn to create the illusion of three dimensional space on a two dimensional surface. Perspective includes dimension, distance, and the relationship of objects to each other. If an artist wants to render a realistic image from a picture or a live model, he or she will assign proper proportion and spacing to create the picture.

One technique used to capture perspective is to establish the vanishing point—the one place at which all things converge. The vanishing point in human life might be the end of life and may be defined by how we want to be remembered after our death. By using perspective we are able to bring to life our two-dimensional "wish" for our future through the subtle choices we make each day in our three dimensional world. All lines of our life lead to this point in order for the picture to make the sense we intend.

Our experiences and emotions don't vanish but converge to "add up" to the sum of our lives. We can go about having learning experiences, adjusting our vanishing point and redrawing our lines. Or we can follow all emotions without choosing an end result and discover that we have ended up where we don't want to be. Learning, adjusting and redrawing our choices are acts of courage.

The idea of determining our own vanishing point allows us the choice to adjust our perspective. That choice will ultimately define the final appearance of the picture. We determine if our eye level is high above and detached, at ground level in the middle of things, or off to the side with a unique point of view. Unlike a picture, however, in life you can adjust your vanishing point each day, or with each phase of your life, as you take in new information and adjust to factors beyond your control. The end goal may not change, but, you can change course to respond to unexpected situations and circumstances. Thus, perspective is a technique of subtle changes to bring your end point into the reality of your three dimensional life.

Perspective seems easy when the picture is finished—when the goal has been achieved or the dream realized. However, when you are developing your life plan, building your dreams, or trying to get through the day, creating perspective can be hard. Selecting a vanishing point and determining how each action you choose moves you out to that point, challenges your trust in yourself. Selecting a vanishing point in the unknown future causes fear because no matter how good your guess, it's still a guess.

I remember realizing that I would not know if I was a good parent until my children became adults. The picture would be finished and I wouldn't be able to go back and make changes or add experiences. I became very afraid that I would fail and doubted my abilities. Then it occurred to me to choose the vanishing point of having successfully raised two happy, healthy, productive men. I changed my perspective to focus on all that went well and chose to have gratitude for those moments that reinforced the bond with my boys.

With this perspective, I am living in the present, which is the only place we ever really are. And, when I do or say something which is not congruent with raising happy, healthy, productive men I can alter my journey to regain my focus. Staying true to my vanishing point in this case reminds me to not be swayed by the favorable or unfavorable opinion or approval of others. I do recognize validation of my daily choices is not only *not* necessary but, if and when validation happens, it may well not show up for quite some time, if at all.

A friend asked me when fear and doubt vanish. My best answer is that fear and doubt do not disappear in the instant that we equate with the word "vanish"—it is more of a fade. Like constantly washing your thoughts and emotions with the new water of "all good things", fading occurs and a new choice of perspective is allowed.

Three Vanishing Points I Choose

1. My boys are two happy, healthy, successful men

2. A life-long, happy marriage

3. A wonderful, amazing writing and speaking journey

What are Three Vanishing Points you Choose?

1. Healthy family

2. A wonderful long marriage

3. A good career.

Three Good Things...
About a Bad Day

1. You might attention

2. You have someone or something to blame

3. You are comfortable because "bad" days are supported

Choosing a good day sounds so simple. I've read a lot of books on happiness, positive thoughts, and affirmations. The understanding of how it all works has been much easier than the doing. It occurred to me that I needed to understand what makes a day "bad" before I could create and be in control of more "good" days.

I found that I had associated "bad" feelings, or unpleasant emotions, with "bad" days—if I had had my feelings hurt or felt rejected, if I was lonely or confused, if I disappointed myself by not meeting my own expectations, or if I physically didn't feel well. It usually only took one or two of these "bad" events to label an entire day as "bad." This is classic "all or nothing" thinking. If you could measure, in a measuring cup or on a kitchen scale, the true quantity of "good" and "bad" occurrences or emotions in any given day, very few times would "bad" outweigh the "good" for most of us. It is our perception that weights the "bad" unevenly. "Bad" is given more focus when we attach current events to past thoughts and beliefs that may or may not have been true, but definitely no longer exist.

In my own life, long, long ago, I received a notice from my credit card company stating that I needed to become current on my payments in order to continue using the card. Thinking that the letter must have crossed paths with my payment, I didn't hesitate to hand the card to the clerk at the children's shoe store. After calling for authorization, the clerk cut up my card and requested another form of payment. End of the credit card, but not the end of the story. I carried that embarrassing, painful scene in my memory for years.

Now, fast forward to current times. Let's say I am not awarded a contract for which I have bid. The truth is, not winning a specific contract for work has no deep or hidden meaning. It's just an event. Nevertheless, I may opt to laden that event with the emotions from the destroyed credit card experience. However, if I choose, I can view the unsuccessful bid for a contract as the simple event I know it to be. Now that it is just an event, I can choose the label I wish to apply. It can be "good" because I will have saved time that I would have spent preparing for and presenting the work involved in the contract. Now I also see that I am free to accept an even better offer, spend more time with my family, or work on another project I've set aside. I have left the "old" baggage and proceeded with my life under the banner of one more "good" thing which happened to me today.

As objective and independent as emotions feel, they are subjective and within our control. Or to put it another way, emotions are our choice; we can choose how we feel. I keep the following equation in my mind to remind me that I choose the thought, or "label."

Emotion = Event + Thought

Our thoughts about an event are what drive our emotions, not the event itself. Not getting a job, eating an entire box of cookies, or arguing with someone we love are all events. How we choose to think about each of them—usually based on past experience—drives our beliefs and expectations, which trigger our emotions. When the phrase "this is bad" enters our mind, the emotional selection process has chosen "bad" as the appropriate label for the event, and this thought and resulting label translate into a feeling. Thus, when the label "bad" is affixed, the corresponding feeling is unpleasant.

Taken a step further, a "bad" day ends up being a culmination of choices based on past experiences, emotional labeling, expectations, and perspective. Pretty complicated stuff for a small three-letter word we carelessly throw around. In the book *Happiness in a Storm*, which concerns facing illness as a healthy survivor, Wendy Harpham, M.D., says that having negative feelings is not always "bad". "Feeling fear, anger, and other negative emotions shows that you understand what is going on." (*Happiness in a Storm*, 198) Anger and discomfort can be catalysts to make life changes or to confront a long standing issue which in the end, results in more "good" days.

A tough thing to face is that there may be benefits to having a "bad" day. None of us consciously wants to feel bad, but we must be getting something out of it if we choose this perspective. We know it's a choice because all of us have heard stories about people who express hope and enjoy each day while living in awful circumstances or dying of a painful disease. So, it is probable that we are gaining something when we choose to focus on the negative.

If I am honest with myself, I see that having a "bad" day allows me an excuse to feel sorry for myself and blame others. It feels much easier than taking responsibility and making changes, or putting a new plan into action. There's something about complaining that also makes me feel like I get more attention; I believe that people might not notice me if I'm not miserable and whining. Take being sick with a cold, for example; when I complain throughout the day, maybe my family, friends, and coworkers will notice me. Maybe they occasionally ask if I feel better, offer to bring me food, or stay extra quiet so I can rest. I like the attention. Additonally, if I don't complain, will they know I'm there?

It's also culturally acceptable to have a "bad" day and let everyone know about it. Others may join in and share their bad news and misery, thus supporting our perspective of lack of control and allowing us to avoid taking responsibility for our choice to be happy. We look suspiciously at people who are "too happy." We wonder what is really wrong with them and perhaps even suspect they are lying about their true emotional state. "No one could be that happy," is what we tell ourselves. Choosing a "good" day may cause us feel like the person who doesn't fit in, and this makes us much less comfortable than we would feel if we shared the opinions of the rest of the group.

Understanding how you benefit from having a "bad" day is a difficult exercise in facing your fears and feelings of uncertainty. But if you truly want relief from a negative perspective, owning your benefit is a first step.

Three Benefits for Me from Having a Bad Day

1. An excuse to overeat

2. An excuse to be crabby

3. I have a sob story to tell anyone who will listen... maybe I'll get more attention!

Three Benefits for You from Having a Bad Day

1. over eat

2. get mad

3. be alone

What Makes Any Day a Good Day

Three Good Things...
About Any Day

1. It's your choice

2. Your values are your compass

3. Perspective adjustment is possible

I have often made the statement, "I hate winter." It's true I dislike cloudy days, being cold, and feeling cooped up inside. And living in a cold northern state like Michigan, I resign myself to repeating the mantra "I hate winter" for almost six months of every year. Since I am convinced that the tool of perspective puts the labels "good" and "bad" under my control, I decided to change the label I had assigned to winter.

I have learned that the energy I previously invested in hating an entire season did not align with my personal values of loving nature, appreciating simple things and maintaining a positive approach. The incongruence between my winter perspective and my personal truth resulted in a misalignment with my value system. Needless to say, misalignment of anything—values, the front end of your car, your hips or back—results in discomfort. I decided to make a list of all the things I like about winter, although it seemed like a daunting task given my perspective. What could possibly be positive about winter?

As I began writing, I was surprised that the items came quickly and before I knew it, I had a list of things I liked about winter. In the winter, it is so much easier to do my grocery shopping between appointments knowing the food will stay cold until I get home. Making the list, I was reminded how I look forward to wearing my favorite hat that fits perfectly and matches my coats. Here is my list.

Things I like about winter

- Icy, snow-covered trees are beautiful
- Holiday lights
- Seeing your breath
- Dark, starlit mornings
- Santa Claus
- My hat
- Groceries stay cold in the car
- Crunching sound of frozen snow under car tires
- No obligation to go outside

I recognize that some people feel that simply being alive makes any day a good day, because of their religious faith or surviving a tragedy. People who have suffered through crisis and almost lost their lives know the value of breathing, heat, electricity, and possibilities. Thankfully, many of us are fortunate enough to have avoided experiencing a serious misfortune. How can we learn from them to provide a new perspective? We can cultivate an appreciation of the basics in life, acknowledge the good in each day, and thus provide a foundation on which to build endless gratitude and peace. Once we have achieved this, it leaves room to want and receive more. The good days will be everything we imagine and more than we dream, even the cold and cloudy good days.

Aligning your perspective with personal truth allows the inner value system to open us up to the good things present in every situation. I was able to test this value system one particular day shortly after I had been diagnosed with a chronic illness. I pulled myself together to meet with an important (but sometimes difficult) client and jump through the hoops which all parents jump through to get children off to school.

While my expectations for the day were not high, I was cautiously optimistic. That optimism quickly evaporated when my client decided to be particularly difficult. Frustration crescendoed until I cried. Yes, I actually cried! I cried in a meeting. In front of adults. They were not my friends or members of my family either. Even as it was taking place, I could not believe it was happening. Through my tears I was still able to marvel at the depth of my humiliation!

Back in my office, the cumulative effect continued. I discovered that a contract on which I had previously bid had been rejected. I had not only bid on it, I desperately wanted and thought I needed it. What could possibly be "good" about a day like I described above?

So, I began to appreciate the simple things. I recalled the nice, warm feelings I had when my husband had brought me a cup of coffee in bed that morning. And, on my way home, I was immersed in feelings of gratefulness as I looked forward to having dinner with my family. Later that evening a friend called, and together we were able to use perspective to review the days happenings so we could laugh about the crying. It was then I realized that my perspective had been turned outward. My personal value system had become misaligned with external approval. The demands of my client, my quest for approval, and even my physical symptoms were outside of my personal truth.

A cultural yardstick would measure that day as a disaster and slap the label "bad" across its square on the calendar. Being able to pick up on the good things about my day was the result of choosing to be in control of my perspective. The things I valued stood out. Many parts of that day were not enjoyable, and I was physically and emotionally uncomfortable. I do not want to discount the reality of the unpleasant events but offer an option to gain perspective.

If left unattended, my perspective may run rampant in the world of "can't", "should", and "oh, poor me". Perspective is a learned response that requires practice and daily attention. Misalignment still happens even after practice and paying attention. The force of ego to win approval, disappointment from unmet expectations, professional set-backs, and a host of other life circumstances put pressure on balance. Being human, we are vulnerable to this pressure and losing our balance, but we can also recognize an imbalance and make corrections.

The chapter that follows tells the story of how I shifted my perspective, and how, to this day, I practice perspective maintenance so that every day is a "good" day.

Three Good Things about Any Day

1. Breathing

2. Heat and electricity... especially air conditioning

3. Possibilities

Three Good Things about Any Day for You!!

1. Smiling

2. relationships.

3. Responsibilities

5

Three Good Things about the Day: My Story

Three Good Things… About Three Good Things

1. It doesn't take much time
2. Anyone can participate
3. The affect is powerful

It's 5:25 p.m. as I pull into the driveway of our new, little, yellow bungalow that at first had looked kind of boxy to me, but that my husband, Mark, had thought was perfect. I can see the big shade tree in the backyard, which has grown taller than the house. We love the backyard, the tree, and the wooden privacy fence. He will be waiting for me. We will begin our daily ritual once again: rush home from our full-time jobs to … *complain*.

We were newly married, still in the early stages of wedded bliss and were supposed to be ecstatically happy, viewing the world through romantic, rose-colored glasses. Despite that premise, our ritual consisted of complaining, gossiping, and poking fun at others' clothes or dating choices. We complained about our jobs, the fact that we deserved better, and how our problems were someone else's fault. No one was safe from our blaming; not the neighbors, not our family, not even people we didn't know. Eventually, gossiping and complaining became our hobby.

This wasn't a problem at first. We would come home after work, complain, eat dinner, complain, watch TV, eat some more, complain, and go to bed. Strangely, we thought our routine was fun even though we had lost our motivation to socialize and assumed we were doomed to follow our lot in life. We were too tired to go out or do much of anything else. It never occurred to us that there was another way.

Mark was a mechanic who put in long hours of hard work for low pay. He worked weekends, and was expected to stay at the shop when there was no work, although he only got paid for the time spent fixing a car. Later, he told me that he felt his situation was hopeless. There were few choices for someone who didn't finish college. He thought he had no other marketable skills, yet he ached for something more.

My work environment was no better. As a secretary in an aluminum plant, I worked for chauvinists who were much less intelligent than I. The Human Resources Director had interviewed me for the job and then introduced me to the Quality Assurance Director as the new Quality Assurance Secretary. I was never formally offered employment and the pay and benefits weren't discussed. "Pleased to meet you" was all that I said, while wondering why I had even applied for a position like this. I too felt trapped, without an ounce of strength to free myself. It's no wonder we complained! The world had dealt us a bad hand and we thought we had to play it out.

I settled into my job and found myself trying to make the best of a challenging situation by organizing a company team to compete in a community corporate athletic challenge. Through that effort, I met new people who worked at my company and from other businesses, and was able to make use of my motivational skills and creative talents. In some small way, I was reminded of why I went to college, and of my dreams for my future.

Then it happened. It was just another typical day, for the most part uneventful. But something had changed. As I arrived home, I had a sinking feeling. I wasn't looking forward to rehashing my day. In fact, I didn't want to call attention to my mistakes anymore. My husband must have felt the same as I did because he snapped at me about dinner the moment I walked in the house. We spent the evening trying to stay out of each other's way (hard to do in our little love bungalow). How did we become so irritating, so boring, and so predictable? It's pretty bad when you get to the point of not being able to stand the love of your life! All of the complaining and gossiping had seeped through our skin and poisoned us with negativity and pessimism. We had become our own worst enemies.

At this time I had a new job but still felt that my life was not in my control. I forced myself to go to work every day. Then I would sit in my car at lunchtime and talk myself into returning to my job. When people would ask what my husband or I did for a living, I was embarrassed and didn't want to tell them. Before we were married, I lost almost 60 pounds, but the weight and the bad feelings were sneaking back. I loved my husband and I had always been proud of myself. How did we get into this state, and at what point did we give up control of our lives?

During a time management seminar at work, the trainer asked the audience to share things that they dreamed of doing but never seemed to have the time to do. I shouted out that I would like the luxury of having time to wash the windows at home. The immediate silence in the room was my first clue that I had missed the point. The trainer asked again and received responses such as go on a cruise, climb a mountain, write a book, and a host of other adventures. I left the workshop feeling numb, except for some residual embarrassment for my public proclamation that my biggest dream was to wash my windows. I knew about dreams and goals, and had always had great vision. My heart hurt with the realization that I had relinquished my power and positive disposition to something outside of myself.

Desperation was the catalyst that sparked my motivation to change. I drove home with a new determined attitude and announced to my husband that neither of us could say anything negative at the end of the day until we had shared at least *Three Good Things*. Our situation felt like an emergency to me, and I knew we had to take back control!

The first day of our new routine was grueling. Mark insisted that there was absolutely nothing positive, in any way, about his day. I stood my ground— *Three Good Things*. There must be at least *Three Good Things*.

"Was your coffee hot?" I asked.

"No!"

"Did someone tell a joke? Did you find a quarter?"

"I know! I saw a deer on my way to work."

"Great! Now two more things."

It took us a long time to complete our lists, even though they were such short ones. We were exhausted, but we still found the energy to complain about our bosses, the coworker who didn't contribute to the team, and the unsuitable size of our paychecks.

Mark now tells me that he thought my idea to look for good things in our miserable lives was some kind of joke. He participated that day because he didn't want to say "no" to me, and I seemed so determined that he felt it was best to go along. My husband has always treated me that way, placing a high priority on what is near and dear to my heart. What I wanted became important to him too, and he went along with me out of loving consideration for what I needed. Maybe the time management seminar humiliation was not the catalyst for my change. Maybe it was the desire to show my love to my husband and pay proper respect to the good things that were in our lives.

Each day we kept sharing our *Three Good Things*, and it became easier and easier. Believe it or not, after a while we couldn't wait to get home to talk about the good things that had taken place during the day. It even got to where we sometimes listed more than three things. Imagine that! Somehow, good things seemed to ambush us throughout the day, hoping to be one of those chosen for our top three. Our attitudes changed too.

We found other people to be interesting, engaging, and intelligent. We noticed the weather and appreciated the sunshine, the thick snowflakes, and even the thunderstorms.

We progressed to the point where when we finished talking about our good things, we no longer felt the need to gossip or complain. We started going for walks and visiting friends instead. And when we found out we were having our first child, we bought a house on Prosperity Street.

Although we remained unhappy with our jobs, we didn't see how to make a change. In the meantime we began to enjoy what we had and see the positives of what we did. It seemed like magic when we suddenly found ourselves with new job choices, yet these new choices didn't appear quite as quickly as we felt they did. We had been celebrating the positives in each day for over a year and we had changed. Looking back, it is obvious how our positive outlooks and optimistic interaction attracted the attention of new employers.

On a wintry workday we met for lunch, Mark and I shared fries and a Diet Coke and talked about a very scary decision. Over the course of 11 years, Mark had interviewed three times with an international corporation that had headquarters in our city. Each time he was told he did not have enough experience or education. On this particular day, he returned from his fourth interview. He had prepared by taking classes, writing an effective resumé, researching the company, and dressing professionally. He confided in me that he was excited, because he felt that this time, he was a perfect match for the position. He wanted that job, even though it would mean a $10,000 pay cut.

Coincidentally and ironically, I had just decided that I couldn't force myself to go to my job any longer. Our second child was 10 months old, and my employer was requiring more time, both days and nights. One evening, as required, I was attending an open house for clients and was situated near a young man who worked in my department. It was then I realized we were being shown off as professional commodities of our company—we were Ken and Barbie! What was I doing there? What could I do? I wanted to escape, but to where? I didn't have another job opportunity.

So, on that wintry day, Mark and I told each other our career desires that would result in our earning less than half of our net income. We weren't sure how we would manage with two kids and a mortgage. The significant part about this event was not the risk or the money, but that we held hands, promised our support for each other, and shared our faith that all would not only be well but that we would prosper. It may sound contrived, but this moment at Burger King® remains one of the most significant moments in our lives. We were completely honest with each other, and in the midst of our honesty we retained a simultaneous optimism that gave us the courage to make big changes.

When Mark returned home, there was a message inviting him to work for the international company. I then announced my decision at my place of business and was promptly asked to leave. Because I couldn't find any flexible work in my field, I had to look elsewhere, and took a job as a teacher at a technical school. With nothing else to fall back on, I gave it a try. It didn't take me long to realize I had stumbled onto my passion.

Changing careers was not the only factor that gave us joy. Our daily dose of sharing *Three Good Things* about the day kept us focused on the positive. *Three Good Things* enhanced our awareness of subtle changes and events that signaled we were moving in the right direction.

My husband had returned to school a few years earlier to complete his degree, but with the age and work experience difference with the other students, he sometimes felt he did not quite fit in. Rightly or wrongly, Mark thought he wasn't smart enough and even though he had a satisfying job at the company he preferred, somehow he felt that he didn't deserve this good thing that had happened to him.

He received a definite signal as he was leaving school one evening. He called me to share it. When the phone rang and I answered it the excitement in Mark's voice made it sound as if he had been running.

"I can do whatever I want!" Mark blurted out.

What was he talking about?

"I'm standing in front of the job board at the college and I can see it. I can do anything!"

I started to cry, and my heart ached with happiness for the love of my life. Infinite possibilities opened up for him as he set aside his past beliefs and finally saw his talents.

Do we never complain or gossip now that we practice *Three Good Things*? Sometimes we do, however happiness and prosperity have become our defining themes. We have new jobs, more friends, less weight, and increased confidence, but most importantly, we enjoy each other's company and the love of our family. While it's true that these changes came from decisions to act, our mindset is what made it possible for us to move forward. Finding *Three Good Things* about each day established the framework for our thoughts and altered our expectations. Now we control our perspective by expecting goods things every day, which is adding up to a lifetime of greatness.

On most nights, the four of us have dinner together and share *Three Good Things* about our day. Our guests are welcome to participate, and often do. A recent guest enthusiastically arrived at dinner with the announcement that she had been choosing her *Three Good Things* all afternoon.

I love our *Three Good Things* time of day. Maybe barbequed chicken has been simmering in the crock pot for hours, and there's that sweet and spicy scent to the kitchen. Broccoli and cauliflower are in the steamer, or corn on the cob is in a bubbling pot on the stove.

The boys get the dishes and silverware and ask if we have any applesauce. Everyone shouts out what they want to drink and whoever has free hands pours the requests. We sit down, each at our regular spot, pass around the food, and share *Three Good Things* about our day.

Our youngest son usually begins, followed by our oldest and then Mark, although he always acts amazed that it's his turn. This is our ritual, and I don't know why, but the boys always vie to be first, with my husband pretending to be surprised. Then it's my turn. I savor last place because I get to hear what is important to the three people I love most in the world. Of course, they are always my three greatest good things.

Only a few minutes each day, you will find, will lead to a culture shift in yourself, your family, and your work. It starts out small like the Grinch's heart, but expands each day. At dinner with family or friends, or even by yourself, you can align your perspective by choosing to focus first on good things. Hearing what matters to others enhances relationships. With this positive energy, the possibilities are boundless. Now, right now, stop reading and think of *Three Good Things* about this day. Take the time to do something for yourself that seems so small but can make a big difference in your life.

Three Good Things about My Day Today

1. Sunshine

2. Walking with my friend Sarah

3. Writing

Three Good Things about Your Day Today

1.

2.

3.

Three Good Things:
Opening Up Possibilities

Three Good Things…
We Expect on Most Days

1. The car will start
2. We will finish the "to do" list
3. The mail will arrive

I n the *Three Good Things* story, I shared how it became easier for Mark and me to find good things about our days. At first, we looked for good things because we knew we would have to share them with each other and, later, with our family. Naturally, we didn't want to be caught without at least three things to share.

Eventually, though, noticing good things about our day stopped being about accountability at the dinner table—it became a personal choice. We expected that at least *Three Good Things* would happen to us each day. This new expectation felt particulary miraculous because, while growing up, I had learned to expect the worst. Like many who have lived in an unpredictable home environment, I had never felt secure in what would happen next. Expecting the worst was a survival and defense mechanism for me, and it served me well until that expectation stopped protecting me and started defining my reality instead.

My expectations continue to drive my reality but they do so in a new way. Hatched from desperation, the *Three Good Things* daily exercise changed my expectations from negative to positive. Looking back, I've tried to pinpoint how many recitations of *Three Good Things* about each day were necessary to change our perspective. Within a few days, we felt happier; within a few weeks, we experienced better relationships with coworkers and friends; and several months later, our jobs changed.

Expectations are tricky because they are dependent on so many things outside of our control such as other people's cooperation and the weather. Expectations are also based on the unstable platform of assumptions from past experiences. What we have learned and experienced so far is really all the information we have to determine what we should or could expect but this information has already been outdated—as quickly as modern technology.

Because expectations can be tricky, they need close monitoring. We often set our expectations like we set goals. We determine specific requirements and plan out a week, month, or year at a time. It is dangerous to predetermine exactly how a situation should play out because we are dealing with the future. Handling expectations with care means they need a short time frame, broad scope, and a lot more attention.

In the Introduction, I shared with you the goal list that became a reality for Mark and me with no attention. Goals are the end result; expectations are the roads we think we must travel to arrive at our destination. You need to pay close attention to your vehicle and your route when you are driving, at the same time being open to alternate routes because detours and side roads my get us to where we are going, more quickly, more easily and more directly than the original route we charted.

Setting your goals for the day—maybe in the form of a "to do" list—is fine, but attaching detailed expectations to that list won't be effective. General expectations are best because they allow more ways for things to happen than we can even comprehend. We may believe that there is only one or two ways to do our work, resolve a conflict, or plan a vacation. But, that's just not true even if we don't know any other options right now. Expecting anything more specific than "good" things limits the possibilities.

Recently, our family was asked to camp with our son's baseball team when they competed in the state championship. We thought we had two choices: borrow Mark's sister's camper or our friend's camper. It turned out that both were unavailable. We panicked because our expectations were not met. Remembering to open ourselves to possibilities, we waited for an idea and trusted that it would all work out exactly as it should. Staring out the window, we noticed our neighbor's camper. We thought they would never loan it to us—we hardly know them—and it's much bigger than borrowing a cup of sugar. But we asked and spent four days in their beautiful camper having a great family adventure. Sometimes, letting go of expectations is required to open yourself up to possibilities you never imagined.

Let's take a look at another example. A friend of mine is quitting smoking. Her goal is to be free from her dependence on cigarettes. Based on her goal, she has expectations. She may expect that she will throw her cigarettes away on Monday and never smoke again. She had this expectation because, in fact, she quit smoking 20 years ago this same way. The problem is, her expectation is based on a past event and circumstances that no longer exist. Is it any surprise that she found herself smoking a cigarette the next day?

Minimizing expectations by shortening their duration and broadening what is acceptable goes a long way toward supporting only "good days". In my friend's case, she decided to begin by not smoking in the house. This allowed her to experience success in the present instead of depending upon a past experience that no longer exists. It was shorter than "forever" and a bit broader in accepting what constitutes success. Sometimes she managed her expectations hourly by dealing with not smoking one hour at a time. All days, whether or not routine, can become the place of miracles when we don't stifle our choices with narrow pre-planning. Letting go of limiting expectations by focusing on the positive desired outcome can allow all good things to happen even in difficult situations.

Managing your expectations allows you more opportunity to affix the "good" label to your day. "Good" does not need to mean "perfect" or "without any bad," but only a weighting toward the favorable, in terms of your perspective. Only a slight tip in the positive—possibly just three small good things—is often all it takes to have a "good" day.

Changing expectations, however, is a lot like losing weight and then maintaining the weight loss. The first pounds go quickly, and the new lifestyle feels fun and exciting. However, continued weight loss and maintenance requires daily attention and is not always fun. Knowing that much of what you expect is actually out of your control can help you let go of rigid expectations and allow experiences to unfold. The weather and other people are not under your control. In fact, the only thing that is truly under your control is you, and sometimes that does not even feel true. When your body is invaded by the flu, for example, you take control of how you respond to the symptoms emotionally though you are not in control of the physical process of the virus.

In addition to the *Three Good Things*, I have added other perspective and expectation managing exercises to my life. Healthy food, physical exercise, rest, purposely meeting new people, traveling, and continuous learning keep me focused on the positive, which includes expecting good things in whatever form they arrive. Being flexible with my expectations is challenging and maintaining my positive perspective requires daily attention. When I feel too tired to share *Three Good Things* about my day, that's exactly when I most need the exercise. People around me would call me a positive, optimistic person, just as they might label someone physically fit. When I have a positive day, no matter what happens, it's because I've done the work to choose my perspective and manage my expectations.

I've had a cold for four days and our oldest son had the flu so badly he has been on the couch for three days. On day five, I awoke, feeling no better. I dreaded having to teach class from 8:00 a.m. until 4:30 p.m. I was still tired from the previous full teaching days while feeling under the weather. Plus, some fatigue had carried over from the previous week, when the youngest member of our family stepped on a nail and developed a blood infection. In addition to nursing him for days, there were doctor visits and medical care. And, I felt something was bothering my husband but he hadn't mentioned it and I was too tired to ask. How could today possibly be a good day?

Nevertheless, today was a great day. Everyone in my class showed up and they were glad to be there. We had scheduled a field trip to the library and the students were so enthusiastic with their independent research that I was able to go home early, leaving them in the hands of a competent librarian. On the way home, I stopped at my favorite coffee shop running into an admired colleague who asked if I had a few minutes to sit and talk. For half an hour, I was engaged in the best conversation about life that I've had in a long time. I doubt we could have scheduled this event.

Later, I was able to spend some time with our oldest son, who was recuperating from his flu, and do some writing. I couldn't wait for dinner to share my good day and hear about the great things that happened to my family. Being tired and worried had taken a back seat to the unexpected joys of teaching, talking, learning, and spending time with our son because I let go of my detailed expectations for the day. By simply expecting a good day, regardless of how it played out, today became a great day.

Three Good Things
I Didn't Expect
about My Day

1. Talking with Ann

2. Enthusiastic and grateful students

3. Time with Erik

Three Good Things You Didn't Expect about Your Day

1.

2.

3.

7

Three Good Things
in All Aspects of Your Life

Three Good Things…
about Your Life

1. Living in line with
   your values

2. Truly knowing your
   family members

3. Appreciating people
   at work

Three *Good Things* helps you choose your vanishing point, align your perspective, and manage your expectations, all of which affect the quality of your relationships. Sharing *Three Good Things* about the day at the dinner table is just a beginning. Your relationship with yourself, your family, and your professional contacts can be greatly enhanced when *Three Good Things* is incorporated in all aspects of your life.

You've read my story and at the end of this book are samples of what my family appreciates about each day. Now, how can this work for you? Reporting the positives of my day to my favorite people keeps me focused on my values, which enhances my relationship with myself. When I've had a hard day or feel off track, this ritual quickly reminds me of my purpose and to live in line with my values. Family is my first priority, but I also have career aspirations and am personally driven to write, teach, and speak. Sometimes, however, living in a social culture that rewards overwork and imbalance I am pulled off track and out of alignment with my values. Practicing daily gratitude through identifying and sharing *Three Good Things* about each day reinforces my chosen perspective and enhances the trust I have in myself to fulfill my purpose.

The other day I was working with a group that suffered from multiple personality conflicts. It was a difficult training session and I had allowed their schedule to take some of my family time. I was feeling overwhelmed with the task of fulfilling my contract within the tension of the group. I did not make my daily call to my husband, and I had arranged for someone else to pick up our kids from school.

When we sat down to dinner that evening, I realized that I was not listening to anyone talk and wished I could just skip dinner and lay down. Our youngest son began to share the good things about his day, and as I forced myself to listen, I found myself relaxing. It was after our oldest son and my husband had their turns that I realized I had detached from my mental dialogue about the struggles of my day and was listening to their good things. Then it was my turn. What would I say? The three things came easily. I was grateful for the beautiful sunshine, the gift of being able to navigate difficult interpersonal relationships, and dinner with my family. I even added a fourth—I am so thankful that *Three Good Things* about the day refocused my energy and attention to what I value most.

This experience taught me to choose work with people who are open to change and not to compromise my family time. Although it is socially acceptable to choose money over family, it causes me to feel out of alignment with my values. That is not to say I don't want to earn an income; I do; but there are many more options than I know. *Three Good Things* helped me to see that I was getting off balance and needed to adjust my choices.

A psychologist friend of mine realized that she needed evening time to work on personal relationships but her schedule required her to work late most nights. She thought if she stopped working evenings, her income would decrease and she would not be able to support herself. Yet, she decided to focus on the positive. Much to her surprise, after she courageously changed her schedule, she attracted new clients and her income increased. This is an example of a positive result that is possible after letting go of a negative perspective of what one thinks will not work.

Sharing *Three Good Things* about each day builds your relationship with yourself and with your family. The *Three Good Things* activity helps family members understand each other better.

I sometimes think I know what my kids will offer as one of their *Three Good Things*, only to discover that what I thought was a sure thing didn't even make their list. I learn a lot about my family from what they remember at the end of the day as being most significant. I have learned that we each get a great deal of joy from being there for each other. For example, our youngest son's soccer goals show up on his list, and on my husband's and on mine, too. The dinner we share each day is also a common item that appears on all four lists. We have a tremendous impact on one another.

When he was 14, our oldest son, Erik, shared with my husband and me that kids at school complain about their parents, but even when he's not happy with us, he doesn't feel the need to complain. "I like you guys," he commented.

"*Three Good Things* about the day has helped me get to know you as people." He also shared that our daily ritual makes the demands of school, teachers, and occasional mood swings (his words!) better.

Getting ideas for birthday presents and learning about what we do at work are some of the biggest practical benefits of sharing *Three Good Things* about our day, according to our younger son, Evan. Birthday present ideas are the result of truly knowing someone, so knowing that mom loves flowers, wouldn't it be cool to get her flower seeds for her birthday. Or, the kids' video game controllers have a worn out button and they tell us about losing an easy game. Hmmm, maybe the Easter Bunny will choose a new controller over more candy. The response on Easter morning is a gasp, followed by, "How did you know!?"

Evan also says he knows what we do at work because of what we share from our list. Our oldest son had a friend who lived in our town for only six months before moving to the West Coast. His family had lived in many different locations across the United States because of his father's work. I asked him what kind of work his dad did and he didn't know. I couldn't imagine him not knowing when the whole family was so affected and because this work was the reason this young man had never developed a long-term relationship with a friend from school or in his neighborhood.

When I talk to other parents, they tell me that the most descriptive words they get from their children at the end of the day are "fine" and "nothing" in response to their questions about how their day went. Maybe they should be asking different questions. Maybe they need only ask: "What were the three best things about your day?"

Professionally, it is culturally acceptable to believe we can and should leave our personal life at home when we go to work. Work relationships suffer because we don't feel free to share ourselves or are not given the opportunity. Trashy talk at the watercooler and gossip in the lunchroom do not constitute sharing of personal selves to our own betterment and that of our work. The sharing I am talking about involves gratitude and appreciation of ourselves and others.

I modify the *Three Good Things* exercise when I use it to address decision making, communication, and workplace culture in trainings and seminars. In seminars that pertain to working in groups, I will demonstrate the exercise and discuss the benefits. Then I ask: "What if you began every staff meeting, board meeting, and collaborative planning session with *Three Good Things* that each person or the organization has accomplished in regard to the group's mission?"

I have seen what happens as a result. A positive tone is established and permeates the session. The group focuses on and celebrates accomplishments. Each member of the group learns about things going on around them—things that would have ordinarily gone unnoticed. They get to know their coworkers, leaders, and organization better, and feel a sense of value and connectedness.

If the culture of an organization is positive, the energy that results from formally sharing good things about work will propel the team to another level. The commitment to the organization's mission and purpose will deepen as feelings of excitement and creativity soar. If the culture of an organization slants toward the negative, or is clearly negative, the initial reaction to sharing positive things may be one of discomfort because it goes against the cultural norm. However, if continued, sharing accomplishments and focusing on the positive will shift the culture in a positive direction.

One newly formed organization struggled with a mix of strong personalities and few shared experiences. The stress of creating a new company and working toward accomplishing ambitious goals resulted in much miscommunication and heated conflicts during planning sessions. Sharing three accomplishments at the start of each planning meeting helped the team members get to know and understand each person's challenges. They were also able to begin each new session on a positive note and move forward from a place of better understanding.

I am still in awe of people's reactions when I tell our family's story in a classroom or a training session. Silence pervades the group and their energy becomes heightened. The common saying about simple things often being the most powerful is so true in this case. Sharing *Three Good Things* about the day sounds silly even to me sometimes and then I remember how my relationships with myself, my family, and those with whom I work have been transformed.

My reason for sharing my family's ritual is to show the power that our frame of reference and perspective has on our level of happiness. It is the smallest things, as Malcolm Gladwell shows us in *The Tipping Point*, that make monumental changes. Daily gratitude of *Three Good Things* sustains decisions and tips your perspective to the positive. You can decide to lose weight or quit smoking but that resolve will not be sustainable without daily maintenance of that decision. You can choose to focus on the positive, but again, daily maintenance is required to keep you from quickly returning to criticism and judgment. Can simply stating *Three Good Things* about your day, every day, cause a personal or organizational culture shift? Yes, it can.

You can write down *Three Good Things* about the day for yourself in a journal, or privately identify your things each day in some other way. Sharing your gratitude with others—family, friends, coworkers, has a different effect. Public declaration of good things is a formal commitment, and energy is shared as *Three Good Things* multiply with each person's contribution. The group creates the culture of positive awareness and the group's energy is infectious. A group can reinforce the ritual and support the culture when individuals are unable to produce the energy themselves. For example, the other day our oldest son did not want to share anything, let alone good things. Since sharing is not forced, we each took turns identifying when we had noticed him experiencing something that might make a *Three Good Things* list. Erik later concurred with our observations of his day and said he felt better remembering those moments.

Listing and sharing *Three Good Things* about the day is not always easy but it is always good. The boys talk about starting this ritual with their own families and about how we'll continue when we don't live together in the same house anymore. *Three Good Things* started as a temporary, emergency intervention to get two adults back on the right track, but continues to be an amazing and powerful tool to create and maintain happiness.

When I went away for a couple of days, I left the following notes for my three men and they then left a note for me when I returned. *Three Good Things* is versatile and can go wherever you go, enhancing your days and all your relationships.

My Notes to my family:

Three Things I Love about My Husband

1. Smartest person I know

2. Loves nature and being active

3. Crazy sense of humor

Honey, you are the whole package.
I love you,
E.

Three Things I Love about Evan

1. Most caring person I know

2. Love of nature and outdoors

3. Sense of humor... ha, ha, ha

I love you,
Mom

Three Things I Love about Erik

1. Sense of humor

2. Self confidence

3. Superior intelligence

And too handsome for words!

I love you,
Mom

What they left for me:

What We Love about Mom

1. She is very understanding

2. She supports me in my sports

3. You are the LOVE of my life!

We love you!

Evan, Erik, Dad

Why I Share Three Good Things

1. Keep a positive perspective

2. Understand the people around me

3. Share myself with others

Why Would You Share Three Good Things?

1.

2.

3.

Three Good Things
at Work

Three Good Things…
About Work

1. **Challenges and obstacles become possibilities**

2. **Work can feel easy**

3. **Work is a natural expression of our "selves"**

After sharing *Three Good Things* at the dinner table people want to bring the exercise into their work environment. In the past chapter, I gave some examples of using *Three Good Things* at work to build professional relationships. In this chapter, I will share how I started using the exercise at work and examples of the impact along with more applications. Since work is an expression of ourselves; it is an important place to strengthen our relationship with ourself and those with whom we create. Too many work environments diminish people by supporting a negative culture of incongruent messages and actions. Applying active gratitude at work can cause a major shift in perspective not only for you but also those around you.

My first public sharing of *Three Good Things* occurred when I helped a committee make a decision and carry out the solution to meet the goals of the organization. As we began the process with brainstorming, the participants interjected comments such as "we really don't have enough money", "well, we don't know if we'll have the same help available as last year", "management never supports our ideas", and "we've tried that before, and it didn't work". I knew, as an outsider, I was in the most precarious position in the room. Who would they blame when the solution didn't work? And, it wasn't going to work because they didn't believe it would.

I stopped the brainstorming and shared the *Three Good Things* story. I described my life with my husband before we discovered *Three Good Things*, our first *Three Good Things* experience, and the changes we experienced as a result of choosing a positive perspective. The energy in the room shifted from frustration to optimism. When we resumed brainstorming, the comments transformed to what could be done, what resources were available and the number of skills and talents on the current team. Although I told the story to remove myself from the hot seat, *Three Good Things* did much more than distract the team from their fears. *Three Good Things* helped them rise above their negative beliefs and choose to see the possibilities.

The truth is there are obstacles and challenges we would rather do without when we are trying to get our job done. Focusing on the negative, however, causes these obstacles and challenges to grow. The process of paying attention to the negative heightens the challenges adding a cosmic exclamation point to our worries. Fear and tension rise and problem solving and creative insight diminish. This happens, not because the challenges are too great, but because we think they are and by focusing on the negative we create the circumstances to support our belief.

Just sharing the *Three Good Things* story with this work committee, without having anyone practice the exercise, was enough to flip the switch, move past doubt and pessimism, and get on with the business of getting "it" done. Was this team successful? Oh, yes! They surpassed their goal a little over half way through the time line. Challenges did come up but the positive momentum pushed them through, over and around the obstacles while they learned new approaches and strengthened team relationships. The work became fun, not like "work" at all.

Since then, I use *Three Good Things* in all of my work. Sometimes it is obvious; we share *Three Good Things* about what we have accomplished at the beginning of each project meeting. Sometimes it is more subtle, by putting "successes" on the agenda before "challenges" or simply giving no attention to a comment that comes from a negative perspective. I do not believe that possible challenges and real resource constraints should be ignored, as if we can do whatever we want whenever we want disregarding potential impact. Moving forward from a positive perspective in a work environment means pushing the envelope as long as it feels positive and then problem solving from an "it can be" belief instead of a negative limiting perspective.

For example, a team might determine their vision requires a new product line to reach their technology savvy customers. An honest review tells them they do not have the infrastructure in place to install a full product line at this point so they move forward a piece at a time and as they do, resources and new ideas come to them so they are able to take the next step. Disregarding the real challenges and plowing ahead with a complete product line would have moved the whole company way outside its comfort zone, instead of just beyond the edge of comfort. This could have caused irreparable damage to the company's stability which is irresponsible to the employees, clients and community. By acknowledging present limitations with a positive focus on organizational vision, answers and resources become clear. "Work" means "hard" to most of us which brings up the belief that if something comes easy then we somehow didn't deserve it or it was a fluke. Work is effort but with positive fuel, work is a natural extension of ourselves, which should feel natural and exhilarating.

I use *Three Good Things* to keep my professional compass set to my vision. When I am faced with a challenge and the only possibilities I can see are not what I want, *Three Good Things* reminds me that what is in front of me is only the tip of the iceberg. In other words, what I can see and what I "know" right now doesn't have to be a perfect fit. If I make one purposeful decision after another, moving positively toward my vision, options and resources will be revealed.

Sometimes, there are several days when nothing changes and I start to feel as if I am resigned to the choices in front of me. Discouragement knocks and disappointment shows up but shifting the focus to the "good" opens my perspective and new choices appear. In fact, one day can change everything. On several occasions many options cascaded into a single day and I couldn't believe that so much was resolved and changed in such a short time!

You know when you buy a new car or a new outfit that you think is unique and then drive it off the lot or wear it to a party, suddenly you see it everywhere? Those cars and out-fits were not there in abundance until you bought yours, so where did they come from? They were always there but your perspective was focused somewhere else and when you tuned it in, they showed up. The same is true for possibilities. If you maintain your focus on the "good", the sky will open and more "good" will rain down. The trick is to keep the positive focus even when it seems like nothing is going right. *Three Good Things* about your day, *Three Good Things* that the team accomplished, *Three Good Things* that will happen when your vision is realized will keep the energy positive, no matter what the external circumstances.

Since the first edition of *Three Good Things*, people have written and talked to me about *Three Good Things* in all aspects of their lives and have been especially amazed at the impact of this simple exercise in their work. One woman shared that she was at odds with a coworker who could not get a weekly report in on time and each week they battled with each other and each week the report was late. When her work team began sharing *Three Good Things* they had each accomplished at the start of project meetings, she listened to the list from this coworker and grew to admire his talents.

She decided to talk to him about the report, something she had never done before, and discovered that her request was not compatible with the company computer system. Her coworker spent hours each week on her request, just the opposite of the neglect she assumed. Together they came up with a report that met her needs and worked with the current technology. Now the report is on time and the two are friendly and have worked through other department problems from their perspective of "good" and mutual respect.

Another person shared that the negative environment of her workplace made it difficult for her to be happy at home because she brought the weight of gossip and complaining home from work. She decided not to participate in the gossip and only verbalize the "good" during the work day. In particular, the new boss was the target of negativity. Initially, her coworkers laughed at her positive comments about the boss but eventually a few others joined in to share what was good about the leader. The energy began to shift and the negativity no longer had enough fuel to sustain. The leader became more effective due to positive expectations and perceptions from her staff. Productivity increased and absenteeism went down.

An organization in a competitive market explored the benefits of expecting the worst and choosing a label of "bad" to uncover what the team needed to move ahead. Through exploring the benefits of being negative, they realized they feared management would not support new ideas and they would be "hung out to dry". Therefore, they used negativity to sabotage new efforts in order to protect themselves from what they perceived to be inevitable failure and punishment. Leadership was unaware of this belief, as were the employees, and all welcomed the realization. Support mechanisms and positive communication methods were put in place to welcome and provide guidance for new ideas. The team felt safe and was able to move forward. Their need for safety was addressed in a positive way and there was no longer a benefit to expecting the worst.

My friend, Heather, is a kindergarten teacher in a busy elementary school. She couldn't think of how to incorporate *Three Good Things* at work. We brainstormed and came up with a *Three Good Things* chart posted in the teacher's lounge each Friday. Teachers and administrators could write down good things on the chart throughout the day. Heather commented that "not waiting in line to use the bathroom" and "compliment from a parent" would be good things. At the end of the day, the group would have a pile of good things to fuel a positive perspective throughout the next week.

I don't recommend asking people to share *Three Good Things* about their day during work. At home is the best place for your personal list. However, asking people to share *Three Good Things* they accomplished, *Three Good Things* they are most proud of professionally, or *Three Good Things* each team member wishes to see the team accomplish offers an opportunity to work from a position of "good". You will move forward from a place of possibility and abundance instead of constraint and lack.

And, people feel acknowledged and proud when they share *Three Good Things*. I have only met two or three people in my lifetime who are completely satisfied with the amount of attention and recognition they receive at work. *Three Good Things* is an opportunity to build self esteem, team relationships and positive organizational culture. It is an opportunity to recognize and celebrate some small but very important accomplishments we often overlook.

I have a client who ends every e-mail she sends to me with *Three Good Things* about her day at work. The tone of the e-mail is always hopeful even when there is a concern and the pride she feels for her work is obvious. From this perspective, we share a positive approach knowing each of us is doing our best and everything will work out exactly as it should. Work truly becomes an extension of ourselves and our values. With the infusion of *Three Good Things*, our product has a positive affect on all who come into contact with our work inside and outside our organization.

Three Things I Love About Work

1. Meeting new people

2. Helping people realize their vision

3. The adventures that obstacles & challenges bring

Three Things You Love About Work

1. Helping people in need.

2. Using my brain.

3. making a difference

Choosing Only Good Days

Three Good Things...
About Choosing "Good"

1. A small shift is all it takes

2. "Good" will become the norm

3. Simple gratitude had great power

Perspective influences perception and expectations, and thus perspective drives whether a day is labeled "good" or "bad". Having only good days and no more bad days is a matter of changing perspective and expectations. It can be as simple as walking to the other side of the room and seeing things from a different angle. But mostly it's not that simple in real life because then we would appreciate every day as it happened and not have to wait months or years to recognize a good day.

While teaching a college class and trying to explain perspective, I knew by the students' blank stares they weren't grasping the concept. I asked them to describe what they saw in the room and make a list. Then I asked them to stand up, move their chairs and sit down to view the room at an angle different than from where they sat when they made the first list. They each made a different list of what they saw. Thus, the same room, containing the same people caused the two lists to be different. The same thing happens with us. Sometimes even a slight physical or emotional shift, usually outside the routine, will allow another option or perspective to be seen.

Too often, however, someone or something has to force us to move from our vantage point. It is very easy, probably human nature, to see ourselves at the center of everything without realizing that the center is usually located somewhere very far from us. After experiencing a change in perspective, the students had a better understanding of their limited view from where they sat originally; that enabled them to perceive the concept of perspective and fully participate in the discussion.

I once went to a staff retreat as an employee of a technical school. It was relaxing and interesting, though a bit predictable until the speaker shared an analogy about our affinity for our problems. She said that when people say, "I wish I had your problems!" or "I'll trade you problems," they don't realize what they are saying. She went on to say that if we were able to put all of our problems in a brown paper sack and set them on the table, and each person was able to select any bag, we would choose our own bag! We may not like our problems, but we have adapted. The same is true for our perception, which is the lens through which we view our life. We are comfortable with our vantage point. We may not have the best view, and may constantly miss things or experience unnecessary misery, but the seat is familiar and fits our fanny. To get up, move to the other side of the room and change our view, is, at the very least, uncomfortable.

Sporadically, I have kept a journal. Visiting entries of 13 years ago, the feelings and desires I am reading about are familiar because they are still true. I cringe when I read some of the same problems I face today. I wonder why I haven't let go. I wonder if I love my problems. I don't love the feelings and struggles, but I have adapted and my problems feel like well-worn shoes—comfortable, but lacking the support I need. Changing perspective requires another level of discomfort until a new comfort is established.

Author Louise Hay in *You Can Heal Your Life* introduced me to how my perception is powered by my thoughts. As I

first read about how to change my thinking through affirmations—powerful thoughts that affect your choice of
emotion—I was doubtful. But I was committed to expand-
ing my *Three Good Things* to experience all things as good.
Louise shares the idea that what you put out into the world
with your thinking is exactly what you experience—you
attract things with your thoughts and emotions. So I guess
it's true that you should be careful about what you ask for, or
think about, and of course, expect.

Positive thinking and the effects of the power of sending our
requests out into the world are truly amazing. One of the key
people in my life is a fellow artist who creates new ideas with
me. We decided to meet for lunch and chose a halfway point.
I commented that it is always crowded in that restaurant and
I wanted my time with her to be peaceful. My friend said she
would go early and check it out, and if it was too crowded we
would go to the less tasty but quieter place next door.

When I arrived, the first thing I noticed was the quiet and
then the darkness. My friend smiled and said, "You got the
peace you asked for." It was a very windy day and a power
line had been knocked down, shutting off electricity to the
entire block. The soup at the café was still hot, but potential
patrons assumed all the stores in the strip mall were closed.
I was delighted and in awe to get exactly what I had asked
for. Trusting yourself and being open to opportunity allows
your requests to be answered, sometimes in unusual and
unexpected ways.

Eliminating "bad" days and experiencing only "good" days is not only possible, but with work it can become the norm. To reach this point you must be willing to put yourself through the discomfort of change. Contentment during adversity may feel odd, and at first you may feel like you are lying to yourself. You might even worry that people will find you strange or uncaring. But think of it as temporary discomfort for permanent peace. This might be one time where "no pain, no gain" is accurate. Choosing a positive perspective creates an experience of peacefulness that expands to calm understanding of yourself and those around you.

The key is to start small. Start by appreciating *Three Good Things* about each day. I am awed by the little things that delight my family. Food is a great example. It is almost guaranteed that a positive food experience will make someone's list. The dinner we are enjoying, a particularly satisfying peanut butter and jelly sandwich, or a birthday cake often takes the number one spot before a gift, field trip, or new purchase. The same is true for a compliment given or graciously accepted. The boys are excited to share how someone recognized their talents before they share receiving a new toy or finding money.

Maybe you shouldn't "sweat the small stuff" but I recommend that you appreciate it. Gratitude for the little gifts open us up to greater possibilities and allow us to choose only "good" days.

Three Good Things
I Appreciate

1. My husband's warm feet

2. A phone call from a friend

3. Hearing our kids laugh

Three Good Things
You Appreciate

1. my wifes smile

2. good friends

3. my little girl.

Three Good Things
Example Lists

The following are examples of a "typical" day at our dinner table. They are in the order in which we present our *Three Good Things*. Evan goes first, then Erik, then Mark and we save the best for last...me!

Evan's List

1. I got to play with Doug after school today

2. We played football in gym class

3. I had pizza for lunch!

Erik's List

1. I got to eat my dads pancakes today; they were great!

2. GOT SOME WORK DONE ON MY VIDEO WITH Z-MAN

3. My brother and I played outside together today and caused mayhem

Mark's List

1. We finished a big project at work

2. I went for a bike ride at lunch

3. All of us at the dinner table together

Erika's list

1. Someone bought a piece of my art!

2. Mark and I went to the grocery store together

3. Dinner with all four of us

Meet my Family

The Oliver Family enjoys the benefits
of sharing *Three Good Things.* In order of appearance,
Mark, Evan, Erik, and Erika.

Ideas for When and How to Use Three Good Things

Three Good Things is versatile and can be altered for many situations, personal, professional or social. Have fun with it and keep it fresh by creating unique variations. I'll share some variations to get you inspired.

Guests: Guests at the dinner table, colleagues in the workplace and friends in a social group all participate in sharing *Three Good Things* about their day, their work or their life. Each guest may opt for speaking first, last, or somewhere in the middle.

Appreciation: Share *Three Good Things* that you appreciate or respect about another person. Perhaps they will wish to do the same with you. This is especially powerful in resolving conflicts, building relationships and strengthening family ties.

Birthdays: Everyone in the group shares three things they admire or appreciate about the birthday person.

Christmas: Draw names as usual and, in addition to being "Santa" to the person whose name each person draws, the giver must also share three good things about the recipient before presenting the gift. This is very helpful if holidays are stressful for extended family relationships.

The Future: To have a good day tomorrow, share *Three Good Things* you expect to happen. It sets up your future perspective to be in line with your values.

Make a Guess: Before someone shares their *Three Good Things* about the day, the others in the group guess what they might say. The guesses may show how much the others know about the person who is sharing and relays their investment in the relationship, even when they guess incorrectly.

Public Relations: Each employee shares three accomplishments and the organization shares the news with the media and key stakeholders.

Wish for the Team: At the end of a planning or work session, each member of the team writes down and then shares three wishes they have for the team. People end a session realizing the importance of the team and the commitment of each member. This activity supports follow through on action items.

Endnote

Thank you for reading *Three Good Things: Happiness Every Day No Matter What!* the "More Good Things" edition and for taking the time to write down your own good things. It is my hope these ideas will help you start conversations about how you choose to see your life. Take time to think about how you could incorporate *Three Good Things* in all areas of your life.

I have had incredible experiences since publication of the first edition of *Three Good Things*. Talking to people about positive communication and working with organizations to enhance their communication capacity has strengtened my happiness. I continue to recover from pessimism but now I have more company. So many people are choosing happiness and as they share their *Three Good Things* experiences, our collective energy to choose only "good" increases.

You will be amazed at the difference that sharing *Three Good Things* about each day will make. Together, all of our shared *Three Good Things* will add up to supporting each other in happiness, every day, no matter what!

Erika's Recommended Reading

- *A Creative Companion: How to Free Your Creative Spirit* and any other book by SARK

- *All I Really Need To Know I Learned In Kindergarten: Uncommon Thoughts on Common Things* by Robert Fulghum

- *Apology: The Importance and Power of Saying "I'm sorry"* by Sheila Quinn Simpson

- *Blink* by Malcolm Galdwell

- *Fight Fatigue* by Mary Ann Bauman, M.D.

- *Say It, See It, Be It: How Visions & Affirmations Will Change Your Life* by Arlene Rosenberg

- *The Call* by Oriah Mountain Dreamer

- *The Dance* by Oriah Mountain Dreamer

- *The Invitation* by Oriah Mountain Dreamer

- *The Power of Intention* by Wayne W. Dyer

- *The Tipping Point* by Malcolm Gladwell

- *What Should I Do With My Life?: The True Story of People Who Answered the Ultimate Question* by Po Bronson

- *Wisdom of the Ages* by Wayne W. Dyer

- *You Can Heal Your Life* by Louise Hay

- *You Can Heal Your Life Companion Book* by Louise Hay

Creative Workshops by Erika K. Oliver

Workshops designed to increase energy and enhance creativity are an excellent way to introduce your organization, association or team to positive communication. Customized content and duration allow workshops to fit into your training, meeting and session schedules. After attending a workshop or keynote address, most groups choose to work with Erika to continue to develop a positive organizational culture and benefits-centered communication resulting in goals achieved and missions realized.

Benefits-Centered Communication: Energizing Your Organization

What do you want people to feel when they work with or come into to your organization? What do you want people to say about your organization? Corporate culture is a choice driven by the behavior and attitudes of the people within it. This workshop will help you see how your corporate personality is conveyed to your customers and community. Explore opportunities to send a message so that it is accurately received, navigate communication barriers, and change your message when it no longer fits the vision.

Three Good Things: Get & Stay Energized!

Many of us think that being tired and busy every day is our only option and there is no way to be peaceful and balanced. In this workshop, you will uncover energy sources and energy drains. Simple techniques will be shared to help you discover and honor your personal mission through creative activities and group discussion.

Whole Brain Decision Making: Activating Intuition

You make hundreds of decisions every day, often quickly and with limited information. Explore your intuitive capacity and learn to use your whole brain to make better and more peaceful decisions. This is an excellent workshop for teams that work together on challenging or long-term projects.

Have Fun at Work!

Explore the definition of "fun", barriers to enjoyment, and the benefits of having fun at work. Share new ways of cultivating joy and creativity at work while maintaining a professional and productive environment.

*For more creative offerings, or to inquire about a personalized workshop or keynote, call: (269) 760-6325 or visit Erika's web site at: **www.erikaoliver.com***

Three Good Things

A Coloring Book for Everyone!

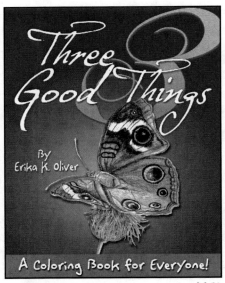

$6.50

Erika K. Oliver has used coloring and drawing to relax and be creative for most of her life. She is a big advocate for adding a little color into life and uses creative techniques in many of her workshops and trainings. Her latest book *Three Good Things: A Coloring Book for Everyone!* allows your logical brain to rest and activates your creativity and intuition. You do not have to be an artist, or even color inside the lines to enjoy and benefit from coloring.

Three Good Things:
Happiness Every Day, No Matter What!

and

Three Good Things:
A Coloring Book for Everyone!

are available in quantity at a discount
from the publisher.

For more about Erika K. Oliver
and her books, please visit:
www.erikaoliver.com

About the Author

Erika K. Oliver is a recovering pessimist with positive tendencies. As a teacher, consultant, speaker and writer, Erika uses creativity to help others express themselves. Believing in personal truth and longing for inner peace, punctuated by laughter, Erika shares the story of how she and her husband took control of their lives, and how they continue to live in line with their values.

Erika, Mark, Erik, and Evan live in Michigan with their two kitties, Peaches and Sassy. They are always at the beach, literally or figuratively.

Erika holds BBA and MPA degrees and works with organizations and groups to set and reach attainable goals. She is also a proud member of the National Speakers Association. You can learn more about and contact Erika at **www.erikaoliver.com**